How To Save
M O N E Y
Buying GROCERIES

Money Saving Tips On Grocery Shopping

Ways To Get Grocery Coupons

by Jazevox

Legal Disclaimer

Table of Contents

Introduction

Eating and grocery shopping usually go hand in hand with each other. We grocery shop for the food that we eat. Most people do both regularly, eat meals and shop for groceries, for as long as we live, for as long as we are alive and living in this planet! No kidding.

Buying food or grocery shopping cost money, and we eat practically every day, so if there are cost-effective ways to shop for groceries or buy food, it would definitely be wise as a consumer to know about them so that we can implement those ways to save money and get the most value for our money. Every little bit of money that we save here and there builds up pretty quickly.

If we have to choose, most of us would probably prefer to save money instead of spend money. But when it comes to grocery shopping we hardly have a choice, we do need to eat regardless, so we have to spend money to buy foods. If there are ways we can save while we spend, why not?

Fortunately, there are ways that we can possibly save while buying groceries! In this book, I will reveal our doable saving methods that we implement regularly in our household.

We work so hard every day to earn money, so if we can keep as much as we can in our piggy bank or wallet, the better. Many of us live our lives paycheck to paycheck. Most of us don't have the luxury of having a disposable income, and therefore are budget conscious and watchful with our spending habits not because we want to but because we have to.

Every dollar not spent is a dollar more left in our pocket. It is always good to find ways to save whatever dollar we can while we shop. Every little bit of savings we accumulate every single day adds up. The more you save, the better!

For those who are on an extremely tight spending budgets, being able to save while grocery shopping could possibly mean being able to buy everything in the shopping list without having to painfully return some needed items that are already in the shopping cart back to the store shelves.

With that said, let's go ahead and explore this book for several ways that you can actually save some money while buying food for you and your family.

Better Way To Create A Shopping List

If you are like many people, then you probably create a grocery shopping list by speedy cramming it or doing the last-minute listing of all the items that you need to buy in the grocery store in a piece of paper. Usually this list creation process happens on the same day that you decide to go grocery shopping, so what usually ended up happening is you cram or rush yourself making such list. Part of this list creation process may involve scanning your pantry, your kitchen counters, your freezer and refrigerator, your cabinets for empty boxes and containers, or anywhere else that could give you a hint of anything else that could be missing in your food supplies.

Although creating a shopping list in this manner could work for some people, it is not a very efficient method. There is a huge tendency that you will overlook some item(s) you might need that may not make it to the list. The worst part is that you usually will not find out about an item missing or being out until later when you are already back home from shopping, and usually not until you finally need it for cooking or preparing a meal.

In the midst of your cooking or preparing a meal, when you finally realize that you are missing a critical ingredient that you need right there and then, then you may ended up in a situation that you will have no other choice but be forced to stop what you are doing and head to the grocery store to buy that one essential ingredient that didn't make it on your shopping list in the first place.

Sadly, I'm speaking from experience, since this exact scenario happened to us multiple times in the past. In other words, I've been there, done that quite a few times myself. Having to go through it can be a very costly and very time consuming undertaking. It can cost money in car gas to run to the store on the last minute unplanned just to get one single ingredient. Not to mention the wasted time it will take to go back and forth to and from the store. The unexpected abrupt halt in your cooking activity eats time as well cause then you have to turn off the burner or the oven for safety reasons, temporarily put perishable ingredients back in the refrigerator so it won't spoil why you are away, close all your windows and doors (if you're alone that time) so that you can go ahead to the store and get that one single ingredient. After all said and done, majority of the time, going through all of these preventable extra hassles will cost you more in gas and time than what the ingredient actually cost.

Creating a shopping list by cramming it is a hit and miss process. There may be countless times that everything you needed made it on your shopping list, but that may not always be the case. Missing something on your list can easily happen in instances like the empty boxes and containers were already thrown away so you have no visual reminders of items that you already ran out of.

Such dilemma can easily be avoided with proper system in place, as far as making a grocery shopping list. Because of this dilemma and the hassle that we experienced going through the same problem more than once that we came up with a better, more efficient method of creating our grocery shopping list that works really well for us nowadays.

In our household, to avoid repeating the same problem of forgetting one item or more in our shopping list, we came up with a better method to create grocery shopping list which I will call an accumulated shopping list creation process. This method seems to work a lot better for us that since we been implementing it we hardly have forgotten ingredients anymore. With all ingredients purchased prior to us needing them, we hardly have interrupted cooking flow anymore. So I can focus solely on the task at hand which is preparing our meal instead of running around the store to buy a missing ingredient or two.

How this shopping list creation works is that we have a dedicated notepad and a pen always available in our kitchen area at all time. As soon as we ran out of any ingredient or any item, we add such item to the list right away. They key is writing the item on the dedicated notepad right away, not later, not after cooking, but right away, as soon as the item come to mind that needs to be bought in our next shopping trip. This way we eliminate any chance of forgetting to write it down on the list which could easily happen if we postpone the writing part. If we wait or procrastinate to write the item down on the notepad until later, then there is a huge tendency that busyness or forgetfulness will get in the way of actually doing it. And then we will ended up in the same old predicament of finding out unavailable ingredients in the midst of our cooking which is what we are trying to avoid and not to occur anymore by changing the way we create our shopping list.

The actual process of actually writing an item or an ingredient on the shopping list or dedicated notepad will only take few seconds. To make this possible, you have to make sure that the notepad and pen will always be accessible in the kitchen for this purpose alone, any time, any day. If there are more than one person in your household, everyone needs to be in the same phase and agree that the notepad and pen has its permanent home in the kitchen area. Make it a rule that everyone in the house has to abide that no one should take such pen and notepad anywhere else in the house and they should only be use for the sole purpose of creating a shopping list.

This method of creating a shopping list is pretty simple process. Writing an item down as soon as something comes to mind as something that you need to buy. Write it down in the shopping list as soon as you realize that you are running out, or out of stock of any ingredient.

It may take a little bit of practice to turn this shopping list creation method into a habit because in order to execute it properly and effectively you will have to stop what you are doing right that moment so that you can write something on the shopping list. But once you get used to it, you will love the much smoother lifestyle of having easy access to everything you need right at your fingertips and feel confident that you can cook without the dreaded missing-ingredient interruptions.

Everyone in your household needs to be involved in this list creation process especially if you are not the only cook in the house. Do not wait for your wife or your husband, or your kids to write an item down. Whoever finds out that an item needs to be on the list, should write it down right away instead of passing this few-seconds task to someone else in the house.

With this accumulated shopping list, your list is basically a work in progress. The number of items listed on it can accumulate as days go by as you add more and more to it. You can add something whenever you realize that you need something, out-of-stock, or running out of stock of whatever item.

You decide when is the right time to go to the grocery store. And when it's finally time to go shopping simply grab your shopping list and shop away. If you purchased all the items in the list, then you can just toss it afterwards. And then start a brand new shopping list as soon as the first item or ingredient that you need at the store come to mind. Rinse and repeat.

Creating a grocery shopping list this way may take a little bit of time getting used to, but it is a very simple process yet very effective and a lot more efficient. It will save you time because you just avoided interruptions during cooking time, meaning you don't have to stop what you are doing and travel to the store anymore. Plus you save gas money by not making multiple trips to the store to buy forgotten items.

How To Avoid Impulse Buy

Impulse buying means buying items that are originally not on your plan of items to buy going into the store. Impulse buying means buying an item that are not listed on your shopping list to begin with. This book is about how to save money, and unplanned purchases are most likely not saving you money, in most cases.

Now that you plan ahead by having an efficient shopping list, as discussed in previous chapter, I highly suggest that you stick to your shopping list to avoid impulse buying.

If you are a regular shopper in a particular store, it is highly likely that you have a rough idea on where everything is located. You probably know where are the different sections of the store are including meat products, canned goods items, fresh produce products, dairy products, snacks and beverages, frozen foods, bread and cakes, etc.

Knowing the different sections of the store can help you avoid impulse buying because whatever is in your shopping list, you can just go directly towards the shopping aisles where each item in your list is located. By doing this, you eliminate the tendency to impulse buy unnecessary items because you are training yourself not to browse all the products in the store and seeing what else is available. Going aisle-to-aisle and browsing through all the products could potentially put you in the want-to-buy-this, want-to-have-that, got-to-have-it, or wow-this-is-cool state of mind, the quick and easy routes to fall into the impulse-buy syndrome.

Most of us have some kind of experience doing impulse buy. To some degree, some people might find it fun to do sometimes, but it can be costly and wasteful spending. Definitely not a good idea when you are on a tight budget going into the store.

Impulse buying is something you usually never plan, as the word impulse implies, it is an unplanned purchase. If you are not watchful and not careful, you can get trapped in a shopping spree that you didn't intend to happen and as a consequence, spending money more than you should.

Majority of supermarkets spent several thousands, if not millions of dollars studying and analyzing consumers' behaviors in order to understand how consumers shop and behave inside a store, including grocery stores.

Every single aisle and shelving unit in the store are usually strategically place with consumers, like you and me, in mind. Most shelves are placed and positioned in specific areas of the store in such a way that products in the store will have optimum exposures to maximize profitability by maximizing every single consumer spending while they are inside the store.

There are usually marketing strategies and greater purpose on how most products are placed and displayed in the store. It may not seems obvious to an untrained eye, but there usually some psychology and strategies at play that will benefit the company's ability to sell more goods to their customers while inside their store. Impulse buying is one of the direct or indirect result of this marketing tactics being implemented.

If you ever noticed, eggs and most dairy products including fresh milk are usually located at the farthest back corner of most grocery stores. There is a reason for that. It is definitely not just a mere coincidence that eggs and fresh milks shelving units are situated in the farthest backend corner.

Eggs and fresh milks are some of the most common commodities among many grocery shoppers that's why eggs and fresh milk usually ended up in the must-buy items in most people's shopping lists. So even if you only went to the grocery store to buy a gallon of fresh milk or a dozen of eggs, you usually find yourself walking all the way to the backend corner of the store in order to grab one, and along the way you hardly have a choice but to pass through all these aisles with shelving units in both sides full of colorful enticing buy-me-too products. A proven tactic that makes people fall for the impulse-buy syndrome.

If you are not careful, you can easily be dragged and fall for these marketing ploys causing you to spend more than you originally planned, causing you to go beyond your grocery shopping budget. Going into the store with a tight budget, it's definitely good to be aware of some of these marketing tactics that many stores implement so that you can shop smarter, stay firm and stick to your shopping list.

You just have to remember that stores including grocery stores are there to run a business. Their main objective is to sell you their products and make a profit. In their eyes, the more you buy the better it is for them. This may sound harsh but majority of the grocery stores probably don't really care much about your tight budget, or they know nothing about how much money you have in your wallet the moment you walk into their store. Coming into a grocery store or supermarket, when was the last time that a store manager or store owner ever asked you about your budget so that they can accommodate it?

If there is one thing most grocery stores and supermarkets do try to accommodate you as much as they can is giving you plenty of options on how you can pay for your purchases. Many stores are willing to accept several forms of payment including cash, check, debit, credit, etc. Stores will not tell you not to use your high interest rate credit cards, their main concern really is that you pay for your purchases. You shop, you pay, and you also take the risk of paying high interest rates later, if you are using credit cards to shop.

So whenever possible, stick to your shopping list to avoid impulse buying. Then you can save money by not buying unnecessary items that you don't need and not suppose to buy.

Why Not Shop Hungry

Shop with a full stomach, in other words, do not shop hungry! This advise may sound absurd to some people especially that for the most part we are consciously aware of our actions, so it is easy to assume that seeing food products in the store when we are hungry or starving will not make us buy foods, or so we thought.

When you are hungry, there is a tendency that you have bigger appetite, not necessarily for specific food but most type of food. When you are hungry or starving, the sight of food products in the store can possibly trigger your appetite that can cause you to start grabbing food products thinking that they will satisfy your current hungry state. Highly likely that none of these foods are actually in your shopping list, so shopping hungry may cause you to impulse buy and therefore will not help you save money because you ended up buying food that you didn't plan to buy and not part of your menu or meal plans.

When you are hungry, you will have the tendency to think largely about food. Going to a grocery stores with a lot of food right in front of you, most of them just a grab away, is a recipe for impulse food purchases. The temptation to buy food items that are not on your shopping list is magnified when your stomach is growling, and food sight will look deliciously appetizing and satisfying , and then you may be tempted to start buying foods to eat later after shopping, well, that's the plan, the new unplanned plan that could mess up your original plan.

To avoid impulse buying of foods you didn't intend to buy, try to shop while your stomach is full, or shop after you eat, then you have much better chance of sticking to your shopping list.

Been there, done that. I admit, I am not immune to this impulse food buying due to going shopping hungry. I still occasionally find myself shopping in a grocery store hungry and majority of the time, I ended up buying either fresh donuts, other unhealthy ready-to-eat snacks, or microwavable frozen meals like Chicken Fettuccini to try to eat later after shopping.

Doing this can sometimes really ruin our meal plans especially when we originally went to the store to buy ingredients for our meal that day. Having these extra unplanned foods that I ended up buying on impulse due to being hungry while shopping can sometimes ruin our original meal plans. By the time I am done eating the impulse-bought foods, I usually don't have much room left in my stomach to eat a full meal, and I ended up spending more money on food that I originally didn't intend to spend during that shopping trip. There were times that I got so full from the impulse-bought foods that I ended up canceling the original meal plan, and the ingredients that I bought that were on the shopping list had to be re-planned for cooking another day.

I'm speaking from experience, this is what can truly possibly happen when you shop hungry. So by all means, avoid shopping hungry!

Worst case scenario, if you don't live alone in your home, regardless if you have full stomach from eating all those impulse-bought foods, you still end up having to cook anyways to feed the rest of the family. There is nothing more frustrating than cooking a delicious food and smelling the appetizing aroma of your cooking for hours in order to feed your family, but sadly you don't have room in your stomach for a single bite!

Calculate, Calculate, Calculate

If you have very specific amount of budget for grocery shopping, having a calculator handy and put it to use can really put your budget in check. There are a lot of portable wallet size calculator that you can easily put in your purse (for women) during shopping. Most cell phones also have built-in calculator, so that would be easy since it is something we easily have access to since most of us don't go anywhere without our cell phones nowadays.

But if your grocery shopping list is encoded in your phone, then it will be a hassle to move back and forth between your shopping list and the calculator. Whereas if your shopping list is written in a piece of paper then it should be easier to use your phone's calculator without switching back and forth.

While grocery shopping, it would help if you can remember the price of each item that you put on your shopping cart, you will find out why later.

Starting with the first item, then the next, be sure to add the price of each item using the calculator. Do this every time you put additional item on your shopping cart in order to monitor the grand total of all items.

If you are in one of the states in the US that requires sales tax, then don't forget to estimate the sales tax, if an item is a non-food item. Also estimate any CRV fees for recyclable plastics and aluminum cans, if applicable. Sales tax varies depending on your state, other countries may have VAT (value added tax).

After you grabbed everything that was in your shopping list and the calculator display a sum that is higher than your allotted budget for that shopping trip, you will then have to decide if you are willing to go over your budget to buy all the items currently on the cart, or you need to eliminate less-needed items and remove them out of the cart. The answer to this decision is entirely up to you depending on your current situation and budget at the time of shopping.

If you can go above your shopping budget and have extra money to spend, it would be easier for you to just buy everything you already put in the cart. However, if you are short on cash or money and going above your budget is just not an option, you can go through every single item in your cart and decide which one stays and which one goes. The best way to decide is determining each item basing on their importance, which items you need to have and which items you can do without.

Whichever item you remove from your shopping cart, don't forget to deduct the price amount of such item from the grand total using the calculator. You can easily do this if you remember the price of each item, as suggested earlier. By deducting the price of an item as you remove them out of the cart, you can easily monitor the new grand total of current items in the cart at all times without the need of entering every single price of all items to get a new total again.

It is a simple method. Add the price if you add something in the cart. Deduct the price if you remove something in the cart. In order to do this accurately, being able to remember the price of each item you grab and put in the cart is ideal. But if you have a long shopping list, it might be hard to remember all the prices. To remedy this dilemma, have a pen handy and jot down the price of each item next to the item in your shopping list. Although, this solution will probably not work well if your shopping list is encoded in your phone.

The good news is you don't have to do this calculation method if you are not worried about going over your shopping budget. Doing this method is a case by case basis. If you are not concern about budget, then this is totally optional and save yourself the extra work and hassle. But not everyone has that luxury of shopping without limit. There may be times that you (or we) end up in a position that you have to stick to your budget with no exception, and if so, then this calculation method will definitely put your budget in check at all times while shopping and will hopefully save yourself from any embarrassment at the cashier's counter in instances that you go over budget and have to cancel some purchases.

How To Utilize Store Newspaper Ads To Save

If you have access to different stores' newspaper ads in which majority of households in the US do on a regular basis because these store ads are conveniently delivered by the mailman in our mailboxes for free, usually twice a month for most grocery and supermarket stores. Having access to these store ads for free is a great saving tool for you, if done properly.

At the comfort of your own home, you can literally compare prices of some specific grocery items that many people buy regularly. The store ads will help you determine which stores have lower prices on specific products. You can compare by type of product, or sometimes even particular brands. Multiple stores can carry the same brands, and sometimes simultaneously advertise their prices of such branded products in the store ads.

If you do brand comparison, be aware of sizes and net weight of specific products since some stores carry customized size / weight / packaging.

Scan your grocery shopping list, then check the store ads to see which stores currently have the items on your list on sale, or which stores have the items at lower prices. Basing on this, add the store name and the price (optional) next to each applicable item in your list, then later re-arrange your shopping list by making a new list according to stores.

Then scan your modified shopping list to determine which stores have the most items with the best deals or at the lowest prices. From there, you can decide to primarily shop in that one store and purchase everything there.

As an option, you can go store hopping, shop from one store to the next, depending on how far apart each of the store are located from each other. You don't want to burn a lot of gas going from store to store just to save a dollar or two. If it would cost you a dollar in gas to go to another store just to save a dollar, then it's not worth the travel.

Another important decision factor that has to be considered before you decide to do store hopping shopping is having frozen foods, refrigerated items, or perishable goods in your shopping list.

It would not be advisable to buy frozen items like ice cream in one store, and then go to another store after that to buy more groceries. Doing this is counter-productive and wasteful because your frozen / perishable items could melt or spoil, and you don't want that to happen. You cannot return such purchased items to the store since it is an easily avoidable circumstance.

If you do decide to go to multiple stores, then the store with frozen and perishable goods will have to be your last stop for best chance of not spoiling your groceries. All your effort of trying to save money shopping will just be out-the-window the moment you start tossing spoiled food away. Remember that you already spent money buying those foods, so throwing them away is equivalent to throwing your money away, and that definitely doesn't save you money in any way.

Discovering Bulk And Clearance Items

There are many clearance items that don't make it in the regular newspaper store ads because there are not enough inventories to accommodate most shoppers, so many stores see no point in making extra effort and spending advertising money on limited-quantity clearance items.

In contrary to going directly to the store sections to buy the items on your shopping list, as discussed in an earlier chapter, in order for you to stay within your budget by only buying items listed on your shopping list to avoid impulse buying. There is, however, a not-so-obvious benefit in doing aisle-to-aisle shopping which is allowing you to discover clearance and bargain prices of products that are unadvertised or unannounced.

There are clearance and bargain products that don't get featured nor displayed in the entrance of the store or in the shelves end caps. A lot of these clearance and bargain products are displayed in their regular shelving locations and the only way you can spot them is by going aisle-to-aisle in order to discover them, if there are any.

Huge markdowns on prices can happen at any time of the year for a variety of reasons including overstocks, in-season products, after-holidays sales, pre-holiday sales when brands compete with each other therefore they undercut each others' prices. When competition between brands and merchants is apparent, the consumers can hugely benefit from much lower prices. This can happen in any categories including meat products, dairy products, canned goods, fresh produce, frozen goods, etc.

When brands and merchants compete with each other, in an effort to entice consumers to buy their product instead of their competitors, one thing they usually do is lower their prices on specific products. The real winners are the buyers because the lower the prices are, the better it is for the consumers' wallet. When brands or companies compete, the buyers benefits the most because such competition usually help keep the prices low, and markdowns are bound to happen to your advantage.

Huge markdown event is something to watch out for in different stores or supermarkets if you want to save a lot of money on groceries that you normally buy at regular price frequently. Some heavily markdown items may be posted in the store paper ads, but that is not always the case.

When you see huge markdowns of products that you buy regularly, this is a great opportunity to stock up on some inventories and fill your pantry with huge savings compare to buying them one by one as you need it.

If you do buy in bulk and stock up your pantry, you need to be aware of shelf life, expiration dates, advance food preparation and proper storing techniques so that you can wisely plan how much inventories you can buy in bulk without resulting in spoiled and expired goods later on.

What is the point in saving money buying in bulk if you will eventually just throw a bunch of the items that you already paid for? It is just a classic example of your hard earn money down the drain.

When bargain and markdown prices are too low of a price to say no to, especially when you are talking 50 to 75 percent off the original price sometimes, it is extremely tempting to just buy all the available inventories even if you feel that you don't have a use or need for it.

Just remember that anything you buy and paid for that you will not be able to use or consume later on is just a waste. So if you buy in bulk, try to make sure that you have ways and means to eventually use the products that you already paid for so that it will not ended up being wasteful spending.

When items are heavily marked down, it will be tempting to buy a lot of it just because they are on sale, but if these are items that you hardly use or never use, the chances of these items ended up being toss or thrown away in the future is highly likely so that defeats the purpose of saving. It is a good practice to only buy what you can actually consume or use. Every dollar you don't spend buying on-sale product is an additional dollar saving, money left in your wallet unspent. What you don't spend, you save, at that point in time.

By not buying bargain products that you don't intend to use, you also give other shoppers the chance to buy and the opportunity to save, in case their household do need those products.

One time, we were able to buy several cans of branded pork and beans for around 25 cents each which would normally cost us a dollar per can at regular price. We bought around three dozens of it which lasted for several months. The shelf life was at least a year, so we had plenty of time to consume them before they expire. Such purchase alone save us a lot of money because it is an item that we regularly buy at full price.

When you go shopping, take into consideration that many products that are easily visible at eye level can cost a lot more to the brands or product companies to have their products displayed at that specific shelving level. For obvious reasons, products at eye level are usually what most people will see first when they go aisle-to-aisle in the store.

So whenever you decide to go aisle-to-aisle shopping, you have much better chance of discovering good deals and bargains by developing a habit of browsing through everything including the upper and lower part of the shelving units as well, not just the products visible at eye-level.

Compare prices and quantities of similar products in order to have a good assessments on which brand or packaging is the best deal for you that will also hopefully meet your product quality standards, as well as your budget.

Benefits Of Joining Warehouse Clubs And Store Memberships

One main perk for joining store clubs and store membership is saving you money. Yes, warehouse clubs including Costco and Sam's Club have yearly membership fee, but they provide exclusive access to wide variety of common household products at discounted prices to its members which can potentially save money while shopping.

If you are currently not a member of any of these warehouse club stores, I am not here to advise you nor am I here to encourage you to join, sign-up and pay for their annual membership fees.

My goal in this chapter is to give you a slight overview and quick inside look of the possible saving benefits of being a member of a warehouse club store. Although, I will only discuss very lightly on the subject of becoming a member, as I will focus primarily on ways to save money while shopping in a warehouse store.

By the end of this chapter, I am hoping that you will have a good assessment of how club members can potentially save while shopping, and some of these tidbits of information will help you decide if becoming a member is right for you or not. Ultimately, it is your decision to make, if you want to join or not. Everyone's shopping needs is different.

After all, this book is about trying to save money while shopping, and becoming a member of a warehouse club store usually requires paying the annual membership fee, and if you don't get it back in savings then it could mean that paying for the membership fee is an additional cost for you.

Majority of items sold in warehouse stores like Costco and Sam's Club are packaged and sold in bulk, and that is where the savings come in because they usually have special deals with different brands and manufacturers to be able to package items in bulk and sell it as one unit to its members at discounted prices in comparison to buying such items individually at local stores.

For instance, Costco may sell a branded peanut butter by pack of two big jars with a price close to a price of one jar in grocery stores. That is like getting the other jar of peanut butter for free! Another possible saving example, is being able to buy a pack for three different boxes of cereals packaged as one for the price of two boxes of cereals at a regular grocery store. That is like buy-two get-one free! The great thing about it is that you can possibly buy such items at that kind of prices at anytime as long as you are a member of the warehouse club, instead of waiting for a sale at other grocery stores.

If you buy a lot of items in a warehouse membership store, the money that you can possibly save can far exceeds the yearly membership fee that you pay. It's not uncommon that this can happen but there is no guarantee either, it all depends on the type of products you would buy in the warehouse club. Some products have bigger amount of savings than others.

Most of these warehouse membership stores also offers different levels of memberships, for example, regular, business, or executive memberships. The type of memberships may be classified basing on the types of perks a member will receive for example, cash back or rebates on your yearly qualified purchases. If you buy a lot of items in a warehouse store, sometimes the cash back rebates alone can almost pay or sometimes surpass the yearly membership fee that you pay, this largely depends on your overall spending in such warehouse store.

Our household has been a member of one of these warehouse club stores for several years because we just couldn't afford to miss having access to these great deals and savings that are offered exclusively to its members. They also have variety of inventories that are exclusively distributed in their store which means that finding exactly the same products in other stores might be close to impossible especially their signature brands.

Warehouse stores like Costco and Sam's Club also offer gas stations (in many locations, if not all), usually with lower gas prices in comparison to public access gas stations. Basing on our experience, the price of gas per gallon are usually lower compare to several different gas stations. Being able to save 5 to 50 cents per gallon by buying gas in a warehouse store gas station instead of a regular gas station can add up pretty quickly especially when you drive your car on a daily or regular basis.

Majority of canned fruits and vegetables and other food products are packaged by the dozen or in bulk but you usually save buying it this way when the price per piece calculates to, let's say, 70 cents per can instead of $1.50 per can if you buy it individually at a regular store.

The key to being able to save money buying in warehouse clubs is buying in bulk or lots because that's how these stores can usually offer you discounted prices and therefore be able to pass the savings to you, as member of the club.

Another great saving opportunity for Costco members is the monthly coupon booklet that Costco regularly send via snail mail to its members. A lot of the coupon savings in the booklet are too good to pass especially on products that we regularly buy. It is not uncommon to save a lot of money by using the coupon deals in the booklet. Getting additional discounts on already discounted products is usually a win-win deals for most buyers.

Store membership programs are not only available to warehouse clubs. Supermarkets like Safeway also have store membership programs that you can opt-in. When you sign-up, you will usually have access to club prices which can sometimes be significantly lower compare to the prices you would pay for the same item shopping in the same store at the same time as a non-member shopper.

There were several instances throughout the year that the prices of their products as a Safeway Club member are 5 to 50 percent lower compare to prices for non-members. Same day, same time, different prices depending largely if you are opt-in as a member or not. Personally, I feel that it is definitely worth it to sign-up and fill-out the application form to have access to much lowers prices of the same products in the same store.

Price Match

As mentioned in an earlier chapter, companies compete with each other to win your business and with that, the real winners are the consumers because companies lower their prices on specific products in a fight to get the buying consumers to buy their products instead of their competitors. Having these type of competition in the marketplace is very healthy for your wallet as the consumer, being the customer with the power to choose where to buy.

In an effort to entice you to buy their products instead of their competitors' products, company usually markdown their prices just to gain your business and shop in their store.

A company's retail business will not thrive if there are no buyers like you and me. There are potential buyers, but they have choices which stores they can shop at. Majority of the time, buyers usually shop at stores that offer them the best deals on products. The stores with the lowest prices on specific products usually ended up attracting the most buyers.

With this on-going competition between multiple stores, prices of different products can be unpredictable as they adjust prices to beat the competition. Store prices on specific products can fluctuate at anytime. One factor that causes this is a store running a sales event on certain products at short period of time. It can be hard for any store to detect when ever their competitors decide to lower prices on specific products and that is where the price match program comes in for your advantage as the buyer.

In a business point of view, a store would much rather prefer that you shop in their store instead of their competitor's store. That's why there are local or supermarket stores like Walmart that is willing to price match the competitor's price whenever you see exactly the same item in their store with lower price at another store.

To avail the price match program, you usually need to present a proof like the competitor's paper ads, showing that they are indeed selling exactly the same product (same brand and size), in order for the store offering the price match program to be able to offer you their product with a price matching the lower price basing on the physical proof that you presented to them at checkout time at the cashier's counter.

With the price match program, the store will usually manually adjust their price for you at checkout. They will not do it unless you ask, so do not forget to ask the cashier. You will need to personally ask the cashier at the time of checkout to perform the price match for you in order to avail the lower price of the competitor. They usually do not do it unless you have a valid proof, so don't forget to bring an actual proof, like another store's newspaper ads showing exactly the same product with lower price on it. It is usually a case-to-case basis, the cashier will validate the proof you will present and decide from there if it will meet the store's criteria for price match.

Most stores with price match program do so willingly lower their price, granted you have the proof, because these stores would much rather have you walk-in and shop in their store than anywhere else, and price match is just one way for them to entice you to do just that.

Even if the store makes very little profit by selling you a product cheaply because of availing the price match program, most of these stores know that if they can just convince you to actually show up in their store and shop there, you are more likely to buy other products that they sell. One of their main objective for being willing to offer you their price match program is to convince you to show up in their store entrance because once you do, they have plenty of other products inside waiting for you to browse and buy. By you showing up in their store, they already won the initial part of the highly competitive battle, which is the battle of winning your business.

What kind of business really wouldn't want to be the one-stop shop for all your grocery shopping needs?

Price Per Unit

If you are in the US, you probably noticed that most big grocery stores and warehouse club stores provide two types of prices in their price labels on most of their products. The main price, printed in bigger font, shows the price that you will pay for an item as packaged, tax usually not yet included. On the same price label, you may have noticed another type of pricing printed on it usually in a much smaller font size, which is usually the price per unit.

For instance, if an item is packaged and sold by the pound, you will see the price per pound as packaged and you may also see the price per ounce of such item which is the price per unit. Having this information readily available to the consumers can help buyers make wise decisions before purchasing. Knowing the price per unit comes extremely useful when a specific type of product is packaged in several different sizes or net weights.

A product maybe packaged as one-pound while at the same time the same item with the same brand maybe packaged and labeled as a two-pounds product. It's easy to assume that buying the two-pound packaging will be a better deal than buying the one-pound package since you are in fact buying more quantity. To know for sure if you are indeed getting a better deal by choosing a particular size or package is by comparing the price breakdown or price per unit of each packaging. The product with the lowest price per unit among the two is the best deal monetary-wise because you get more in quantity (either in counts, weights, etc.).

Having this type of information readily available to consumers without having to manually calculate each item to determine the price per unit, you can easily decide which size packaging or brand names offer you the lowest price of a particular items at quick glance.

Be aware that bigger packaging or more net weight of a specific product doesn't always mean that it is the best deal. With the help of price per unit, you can determine right away which one you should buy if you are shopping for the best price in which you get more for what you paid.

One day I grabbed a bottle of 24-oz catsup in the store shelf. Then I noticed that displayed right next to it was the same brand catsup with 48-oz net weight on it. I immediately grabbed the bigger bottle and returned the smaller bottle in the shelf assuming that the manufacturer is instantly giving me a better deal by buying a bigger size catsup. To make sure, I decided to check the price per unit of both bottles and I realized that buying the smaller bottle ended up being cheaper basing on the price per unit. With the smaller bottle, I would pay less per ounce of catsup. So then I decided to return the 48-oz catsup and bought two bottles of the 24-oz catsup instead.

That was not the first time that bigger packaging ended up being more expensive basing on the price per unit. The truth is in the numbers (price per unit), not the size of packaging or quantity inside. Although, majority of the time, supersize products are usually cheaper by price per unit, personal buying experience suggests that that is not always the case. So if price per unit is provided, utilize it to find the best deal.

If price per unit pricing is not provided in your local grocery store, you can still manually determine the price per unit by doing the calculation yourself. To be able to do this easily, you need a calculator for quick and more accurate calculation, and you need to know some basic unit equivalents, for example, there are 12 pieces in a dozen, or there are 16 ounces in a pound, as these are two of the most common units being use in grocery products.

For example, you are facing an uncertainty trying to figure out which package of chocolate bar is actually cheaper. Is it a one-pound of chocolate bar with a price of $8? Or is it an 8-ounce of mini chocolate bar priced at $2? To calculate the price per unit of the one-pound chocolate bar, divide $8 by 16, considering the fact that one pound equals 16 ounces. The result of the division, also known as quotient, is 0.50, meaning that the price per unit of the one-pound chocolate bar is $0.50 per ounce. To calculate the price per unit of the chocolate mini bar, divide $2 by 8, and the quotient equals 0.25, meaning that the mini chocolate bar cost $0.25 per ounce. Basing on the calculation results of both chocolate bars, one-pound bar and 8-ounce mini bar, the price per unit reveals that buying the 8-ounce bar is cheaper since you will only be paying $0.25 per ounce compare to the one-pound bar which will you cost $0.50 per ounce.

Finding Coupons And Rebates

Be on look-out for coupon books in the mail. A lot of companies grab an advertising spot in many different coupon books to reach millions of consumers on a monthly basis. If you are in the US, you usually get these coupon books for free, delivered straight to your mailbox via the postal service. Majority of these coupon books are distributed to American's household mailboxes for free, so that means most of us who are in the US have access to these coupons for free on a regular basis.

Another great place to find coupons is online. There are reputable coupon and rebate websites that you can browse online that provide printable coupons of different products that you can then print and use to physically present in a brick-and-mortar store to buy specific products.

Just like coupons that you get in the mail, you need to watch out for expiration dates as sometimes expired coupons still show up and viewable online because website owners couldn't remove these expired coupons in their sites on a timely manner, depending on how automated their websites are, not all sites are created equal.

Another great place to find coupons and rebates is in product packaging. Some product packaging and labels have manufacturer's coupons or mail-in rebate forms printed on them. Usually these bonus coupons are not visible unless you buy the product and open the packaging which will then reveal hidden coupons, if there are.

Even though some coupons are hidden and not visible in the outside packaging, majority of the time there is a note in the packaging announcing that there is a coupon or mail-in rebate available inside, and the only way to access such coupons / rebates is if you buy the product. You can then utilize this coupon later on, like getting a discount of specific product on your next shopping trip.

It's also important to note that there are stores that have bonus offers and coupons printed on the sales receipts. Although, not all stores do this, if one of your local grocery store does offer this extra perk for being a shopper, you have to develop a habit of checking your receipts just to make sure that you won't miss any special savings and discounts.

One time, one of my grocery receipts had a coupon appended on it that said $5 off on my next minimum purchase of $50 or more. That means I am getting 10 percent off if I buy $50 worth of groceries on my next shopping trip in that particular store. And since it is one of the store that we buy groceries from regularly, we could easily spend $50 at the store and be able to avail such special offer. A $5 saving is better than none. I can easily buy five cans of pork and beans at regular price with the $5 saving that I didn't have to spend. There are two ways of looking at it, I still have that five dollar residing in my pocket, or I have that five dollar to buy additional foods.

Some stores offer these bonus coupons printed on the receipts as a way to encourage repeat buyers, as well as a means to appreciate their customers loyalty to their store.

Another great place to hunt for coupons is by browsing on social media. Majority of brands or companies nowadays have online presence. Aside from their traditional website, majority of them also have social media pages like Facebook and Twitter. Chances are they posts some time-sensitive deals and coupons in their Facebook or Twitter posts, you will never know unless you check or follow them.

Here is a lesser known secret, majority of the really good discounted offers and coupon deals are hidden inside companies' online newsletters. The only way you can get access to these hidden perks, whenever they do give them out, is by signing up for their online newsletters. The trade off is you will need to give them your email address in exchange for private access to their newsletters. Signing up for newsletter means you will have to deal with whatever information the company will deliver digitally straight to your inbox. There is no way of telling exactly what kind of information they will send to you, that all depends on each company.

There are no guarantees that you will receive special coupons and rebates in their online newsletters. You may or may not get exclusive coupons and rebates from their newsletters. But if some companies do decide to give out those special perks exclusively to their newsletter subscribers, then the only way to have access to those special deals is by being a subscriber. As a subscriber, you are most likely one of the first ones to know whenever such companies will have incoming sales, coupons and rebates available to print in their website, etc. There are companies that do utilize newsletters to give exclusive coupons and special deals to their loyal followers, in this case, signing up for their newsletters, giving you private access to exclusive insider deals that are usually not available and will never be known to the general public.

If you are unsure which companies' online newsletters you want to receive regularly, you can always try to sign-up for as many or as few as you want. After receiving some of their newsletters and you feel that you are not receiving much value or useful information to continue receiving anymore, you can always unsubscribe. Most reputable companies and brands usually honor a subscriber's request to unsubscribe and opt-out meaning they will remove your email address in their mailing list and from then on you should no longer be receiving anymore newsletter from them.

When it comes to rebates, just a friendly reminder, don't forget to mail those mail-in rebate forms in order to actually get the savings that you were after. Some people get excited about mail-in rebates, the savings they will be getting but sometimes forget to do the crucial steps of printing the form, filling in the required information, give copy of the receipt, and mail the form to the specified address for the rebate. If you forget to do these required steps then you are basically paying for an item at regular price, which chances are you probably wouldn't bought if it was not for the enticing rebate.

Now that you know where to find all these coupons, time to use them all! Well, not so fast! With all the coupons readily available out there, it is easy to assume that you are saving money if you get discounted prices in a lot of products by using these coupons. There is a misconception about actually saving money this way. Here is something to think about, just because you can buy it cheaper, doesn't mean that you are saving money because you are buying it at discounted price.

You have to remember that whenever you do buy something you do spend money regardless if it is discounted or not. If an item is not in your shopping list and if it is not something you need, it is best to think twice before actually buying it. Don't let the false concept of saving money by using coupon to buy unnecessary items. Buying items that you don't need at cheaper price doesn't mean that you are actually saving money because you just ended up spending money on items that you don't need in the first place.

There is a huge difference between buying items that you will need and use while using coupons to save money, and buying items on impulse just because there are coupons available to use. Regardless which one, you will still be spending money. By not buying items on impulse, your saving is way greater because you spent none.

Having a coupon of specific brand or product doesn't always mean that you have the best deal available in the market. In order to find out the best deal, you may still want to compare prices from different stores, and check the price per unit (as discussed in previous chapter) for each different brand selling the same type of product.

Price Markdowns On Expiring Goods

There are some stores including Walmart that heavily markdown the prices on some perishable food items like meats. Usually, they markdown the prices when these items are very close to their sale-by-date markings, or expiration dates as indicated in the product labels. Most likely, these stores would rather cut their losses and sell these items super cheap before the products reached the unsellable state like expired date, instead of tossing these products away and have to go through the hassle of safely disposing these items.

Over the years, we have saved a lot of money purchasing some of the meats in this manner. With price of meat nowadays, having these awesome discounts is great.

Although, this type of discount is not always available. Usually, only when stores that do offer these type of discounts, have remaining unsold inventories that are near the sale-by-date labels.

Timing is everything when it comes to finding these type of deals because the inventories are very limited since these products are usually leftovers and running out of stocks.

You are not buying expired goods, these products are just getting closer to their expiration date or sell-by-date labels.

The key to buying these type of products is having a definite plan to be able to use them right away, or if there is a specified use or freeze date in the product label, then you have to make sure that you will be able to freeze the products on or before such specified date to prolong its lifespan a little bit, for meats usually few more months in the freezer.

As mentioned, not all grocery stores offer this type of discount, but if your local grocery store do offer them, this is another great way to save a lot of money on foods that are normally priced a lot higher when you buy them at regular price. This type of discount is usually offered at the meat product section of the store.

If you happen to see a product stocker or store's meat butcher, you might want to take this opportunity to talk the person to know some insider's tips. Ask if they offer these type of discounts and if they do then ask what are the typical days and times you are most likely to catch these discounted products. There is no guarantee that they will share such information to you, but it doesn't hurt to ask and try to gather some money-saving tips.

Grow Your Own Food

I hear you, growing fruits and vegetables sounds like an off-topic for this book, but it really is not. Fruits and vegetables are commonly found among most people's shopping lists for buying at the grocery stores and supermarkets. If fruits and vegetables are never on your shopping list, then that is another story, maybe you don't eat fruits and vegetables, or maybe because you already grow your own fruits and vegetables so you don't need to buy them at the store anymore, just a wild guess!

Fruits and vegetables can be very expensive at the store. That is why growing them is a great alternative and saves you money by not buying them.

Aside from saving money, another great advantage of growing your own fruits and vegetables is that you know exactly the quality of food you feed to your family. If you practice organic gardening then you don't have to worry about chemicals and pesticide contamination in your food harvests.

Many fruit plants grow on trees and will usually need some yard in order to grow them. If this is your first time growing fruits, or you have limited gardening space, I would suggest growing fruits and vegetable plants that you can easily grow on pots and containers including tomatoes, bell peppers, blueberries, strawberries, etc.

Many different types of herbs like basil, rosemary, parsley tend to do very well in pots compare to planting them directly in the ground. Some plants can grow in smaller size gardens or bigger pots with trellis like cucumbers and string beans plants.

Every year, we usually grow a bunch of tomato plants and as a result we have harvested a lot of tomatoes, sometimes more than we can consume in a month or so. To avoid wasting them, we make spaghetti sauce out of them to add to our spaghetti meal, and any extra leftover spaghetti sauce we freeze for later consumption. By doing this, we just avoided letting all these tomatoes rot and throwing them away.

If you don't have a yard to grow your own fruits and vegetables, you might want to check out your local area or city for any community garden nearby in which you can grow fruits and vegetables in a shared garden area with other members of the community.

If you want to know more about growing fruits and vegetables, check out this blog www.GardenersLand.com

Bonus Chapter - Two Smoothie Recipes

Fruits And Vegetables Blend Smoothie

Ingredients:

3/4 - 1 cup fresh or frozen strawberries

3/4 - 1 cup fresh or canned pineapple, include the juice

1 cup carrots, peeled and chopped

2 pieces ripe bananas, peeled

1/2 cup plain or vanilla flavored yogurt, or vanilla ice cream

1/2 cup 100% mango nectar juice (usually, I use Langers brand)

1/2 cup guava nectar juice (usually, I use Kerns brand)

2 cups ice cubes

Serving size : 2 to 3 persons

Instruction:

Add all ingredients in a blender with the ice cubes on top.

Serve right away.

Green Smoothie Recipe

Ingredients:

2 cups organic kale leaves, chopped

1 fresh apple, peeled and chopped, seeds removed

2 pieces ripe bananas, peeled

1/2 cup 100% pure orange juice (any brand works, I usually use Langers brand)

1/2 cup green seedless grapes, or

1/3 cup green grape juice (as an alternative for seedless grapes above)

1 tablespoon grounded organic flax seeds

1 tablespoon organic honey or Agave nectar (as sweetener)

1 to 2 cups ice cubes

Serving size : 2 persons

Instruction:

Add all ingredients in a blender with the ice cubes on top.

Serve right away.

Note: The two BONUS smoothie recipes included in this book are just samplings of our Tropical Smoothie Recipes BOOK that you can buy at Amazon. I have more healthy and delicious smoothie recipes available in our food blog www.HomeyCircle.com

Conclusion

With all the different ways to save money in your grocery shopping mentioned in this book, I hope that you find many, if not all, of them useful that you can hopefully incorporate in your own grocery shopping habits in order to save as much money as you possibly can.

One last thing that I need to point out is that buying products at their cheapest price does not always mean that you are getting the best value for your money. For instance, when you buy fruits and vegetables at the grocery store, it might be considerably cheaper, but you are probably buying produce that are most likely not fresh harvest and were possibly grown using pesticides and other chemicals. On the other hand, buying fruits and vegetables at farmer's market may be a little more expensive price-wise, but the freshness and quality of produce you are getting may be far more superior than the ones available at the grocery store.

Same goes with buying meats. You might be getting a lot cheaper price buying meat at a grocery store, but that doesn't mean that you are getting the best quality of meat. Some stores might be selling meats at a lot higher price but if the animals were grass feed, lived in a roam free unconfined environment before they were humanely slaughtered, then you might be getting a lot more value buying such meat in comparison to buying the cheapest meat that don't have the same quality.

It's not the same for everyone. Depending on your tolerance level, your lifestyle and your choices, what quality of food means to you and your family.

THANK YOU Message

I want to personally THANK YOU for reading this book. I hope that you found some valuable information in this book, and that you learned something useful and helpful by reading this book.

I need a favor from you!

If you found this book helpful and/or informative, please take a minute or two to leave me a review at Amazon, so that others will be able to find or discover this book as well and hopefully can benefit the same information discussed in this book.

Check out my other books, available at Amazon!

https://www.amazon.com/author/jazevox

FREE Home, Food & Lifestyle Newsletter

I will be releasing more books in the near future. Receive an email notification when I release a book. Get free recipes, food and cooking videos and more, sign-up form for the FREE Newsletter available at www.HomeyCircle.com

Sincerely, Jazevox